T0146843

THE PRACTICAL STRATEGIES SERIES
IN GIFTED EDUCATION

series editors
FRANCES A. KARNES & KRISTEN R. STEPHENS

Early Childhood Gifted Education

Nancy B. Hertzog, Ph.D.

Routledge
Taylor & Francis Group

NEW YORK AND LONDON

First published 2008 by Prufrock Press Inc.

Published 2021 by Routledge
605 Third Avenue, New York, NY 10017
2 Park Square, Milton Park, Abingdon, Oxon OX14 4RN

Routledge is an imprint of the Taylor & Francis Group, an informa business

ISBN 13: 978-1-59363-321-9 (pbk)

Contents

Contents

The Practical Strategies Series in Gifted Education offers teachers, counselors, administrators, parents, and other interested parties up-to-date instructional techniques and information on a variety of issues pertinent to the field of gifted education. Each guide addresses a focused topic and is written by scholars with authority on the issue. Several guides have been published. Among the titles are:

- *Acceleration Strategies for Teaching Gifted Learners*
- *Curriculum Compacting: An Easy Start to Differentiating for High-Potential Students*
- *Enrichment Opportunities for Gifted Learners*
- *Independent Study for Gifted Learners*
- *Motivating Gifted Students*
- *Questioning Strategies for Teaching the Gifted*
- *Social & Emotional Teaching Strategies*
- *Using Media & Technology With Gifted Learners*

For a current listing of available guides within the series, please contact Prufrock Press at (800) 998-2208 or visit http://www.prufrock.com.

"The ability to challenge children intellectually is the critical ingredient that differentiates the ordinary classroom from the distinguished one." (Feinburg & Mindess, 1994, p. 83)

Imagine two kindergarten classrooms. It is the first hour of the morning. In the first classroom, the teacher is in the front of the room giving a small group a guided reading lesson while the other children are in their seats quietly completing the "work of the day," which consists of an open-ended journal assignment, a worksheet on letter-sound relationships, a coloring puzzle with basic math facts as the key to the colors, and a worksheet where children practice printing their first and last names. The classroom is fairly quiet, with the teacher's small group providing the conversation. If students finish their work early, they can get a book from the class library and bring it back to their desks until it is their turn to read with the teacher.

In the second classroom, the children are working individually or in small groups on activities of their choice. Some of the children are creating "boxes and junk" representations of the machines they are studying. Another small group of children is writing stories together. Four children are working on the computer. Two are typing stories they wrote the day before, and two are playing a math game together. Two other children are in the class library "buddy reading," where they choose to read a book of their choice to a friend, and another small group of children is working with the teacher to prepare a survey about machines that their families use at home. Some children are building with blocks and others are using special markers at the art center to draw pictures of machines they use every day. When they finish their drawings, they write independently about their machine and what it does, or they dictate their description to a teacher or another child. There is conversation among students in every area of the room. All children are engaged.

Which classroom would create a warm, caring environment for acceptance, risk-taking, growth, and challenge? Which classroom would celebrate the diversity of each child?

This guide provides practical strategies for creating the type of classroom described in the second scenario. In this learning environment, children learn self-direction, have opportunities to express their ideas, get feedback from peers and adults, wrestle with ideas and problem solve, and appreciate the work and ideas of others. In addition, this guide is organized around essential questions that focus our attention and efforts toward how to best educate young children with promising potential or those who exhibit gifted behaviors. Who are these children? How do we challenge them at home and at school? What informs our practices? The practical strategies presented here are for parents, teachers, caregivers, and all of those in the community who are "teachers" of our young children.

Who Are Young Gifted Children?

Gifted education literature includes many lists of characteristics, both positive and negative, of young gifted learners. Early development often is associated with giftedness, but it is not always a determining factor. Parents and teachers should look for signs of advanced development and address specific needs associated with it, but one must be careful not to assume that all children who read early or have strong language skills eventually will be identified as a gifted learner. Language and vocabulary are associated with early childhood environments and can be more advanced in children who have wide exposure to language-rich environments.

One of the most comprehensive compilations of characteristics of young gifted children may be accessed through the Frances A. Karnes Center for Gifted Studies at the University of Southern Mississippi (http://www.usm.edu/gifted/gifted_preschoolers. html). Listed in the Center's *Reaching Potential* brochure (n.d.) are the following cognitive, social, and emotional characteristics that often are seen in gifted preschoolers:

Cognitive Characteristics:
- alertness in infancy,
- faster pace in reaching motor development milestones,
- early language development,
- advanced vocabulary,
- complex speech patterns,
- interest in the alphabet and symbols,
- intense curiosity,
- sustained attention,
- abstract thinker,
- ability to transfer knowledge,
- generates original ideas,
- creative/imaginative,
- excellent memory, and
- may be an early reader.

Social and Emotional Characteristics:
- early empathy development,
- emotional intensity/sensitivity,
- frustration with own limitations,
- concern with truth and fair play,
- early awareness of difference,
- mature sense of humor,
- perfectionism, and
- leader in cooperative play. (p. 2)

Two recent articles in *Gifted Child Today* (Anonymous, 2007; Leigh, 2007) reveal how parents perceive the above characteristics in their own children. One mother states, "To our amazement, a month before his third birthday he could read simple words. It wasn't long before he could read anything he wanted. It was at this point that we realized . . . we were beginning a lifelong search for balance—for him and for the rest of the family" (Anonymous, 2007, p. 21). Another parent notes, "I was concerned that although he was nice to other kids, socially he wasn't necessarily making close friends. He tended to concentrate all his efforts on academics, and I wanted him to be a more well-rounded person" (Leigh, 2007, p. 41).

In both cases, parents mention the positive and negative traits of their gifted children, including the emotional sensitivity that often is associated with very bright children and their difficulty in developing peer relationships because of their advanced academic abilities. Both parents also discuss how other people noticed their child's exceptional characteristics before they did. In both examples, the children were first-born. It may be the case that children's advanced skills and talents go unnoticed in such families because parents do not have opportunities to make comparisons with other children of the same chronological age. Upon entering preschool or childcare, parents begin to see some of the above characteristics because they start to notice differences between their child and his or her peers.

Practical Strategy 1: Value the Competencies of the Young Child

In order to create a warm, nurturing environment where children feel free to express their ideas and seek answers to their questions, adults have to value those ideas. Philosophically, they have to believe that children come to the early childhood classroom filled with valid ideas and questions. To value the competencies of young children is to use their knowledge as the starting point for learning by giving them authentic reasons to learn more by making connections to what they already know.

Young children are remarkably different from one another and unpredictable! They can be rattling off the price of the green beans they notice from the seat of the shopping cart one minute and having a tantrum because their mother did not buy the cookies they wanted the next. Children who are so variable in their intellectual and emotional growth demand special skills of their caregivers, especially patience and flexibility. It's precisely this variability in young children's development that distinguishes the field of early childhood gifted education from its larger context of gifted education. Visualized as the overlap

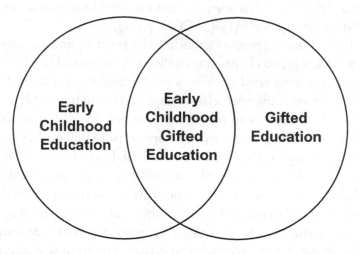

Figure 1. Overlapping of fields of study.

between gifted and early childhood education, it draws its theories and principles from larger fields of study, including human development, learning theories, and cognition (see Figure 1). More importantly, early childhood gifted education's overlap with early childhood general education distinguishes it from the field of gifted education. Early childhood education (ages 3–8) has a strong national organization, the National Association for the Education of Young Children (NAEYC), which defines quality and standards. When educating young children, one must consider the following:

1. the *potential* inherent in all young children;
2. the importance of the home environment and early experiences;
3. the variety of early childhood settings and different types of "teachers" (e.g., home day care, center day care, private preschools, public preschools for children considered at risk); and
4. the relationship between curriculum and instruction and "developmentally appropriate practice."

Practical Strategy 2: Appreciate and Enjoy
the Uniqueness of the Young Child

Parenting literature cautions parents not to compare siblings. In fact, parents sometimes wonder how their own children can have the same parents, because differences between siblings are so pronounced. In an educational setting, teachers need to appreciate the uniqueness of each child in the class in order to foster an attitude of addressing students' different interests and needs, rather than thinking of students collectively as a group at a particular age level.

It is important to take into consideration what is developmentally appropriate for 3- and 4-year-olds, but it should not be assumed that 3- and 4-year-olds are developing all alike or at the same pace. Therefore, teachers and parents should not make assumptions about what the children can or need to do based on what is "typical" for children at specific age levels. For example, during one whole-group meeting in a preschool classroom, the teacher wrote the children's ideas down on Post-it® notes as children brainstormed their experiences with musical instruments. An observer asked why the teacher wrote the ideas down when the children could not read. Her assumption about preschoolers being unable to read was incorrect. Some preschoolers were able to read the responses. More importantly, for those children who were not able to read, they could remember what they had contributed to the group and they could find their own Post-it® note, thereby associating print with language and giving them an authentic reason to pay attention to what was printed on the paper. Writing down the ideas of preschoolers as we would for older children is an appropriate strategy to foster literacy development, although we do not expect every child to have the same response to the printed text.

Assessment and Evaluation of Young Children

All young children have potential that has not yet manifested into gifts and talents. Some young children have talents that are identifiable and recognizable. When talking about young gifted children in the field of early childhood gifted education, both groups must be considered. All children, those whose potential has not yet been realized and those demonstrating a skill, an art, or a mental capacity far beyond what is typical for their chronological age, should be considered.

Young children must be assessed and evaluated to inform adults of the ways their interests, skills, and dispositions toward learning can be nurtured. The manifestation of gifts and talents in young children (like all people) is dependent upon culture, environment, chance, and heredity. The important question in early childhood gifted education is not so much, "Who are the young gifted," but, "How do we identify, foster, and develop the talents of young children?" The focus of assessment in young children therefore, is not to label children gifted and give them the mindset of fixed intelligence, but to encourage young children to have a growth mindset, where ability develops incrementally over time (Dweck, 2006). Most importantly, parents and educators want to instill in young children a love for learning and the dispositions to inquire, reflect, create, and reveal their emerging strengths and talents. Assessment provides the information needed to find entry points that foster engagement and the disposition to learn.

Practical Strategy 3: Become "Listeners" of Young Children

The first tool in assessing the strengths of young children is that of observation. *Newsweek* listed the preschools of Reggio Emilia, Italy, as one of the best models of early childhood education in the world (Kantrowitz & Wingert, 1991). The Reggio Emilia Approach has influenced many schools throughout the world. The National Association for the Education of Young Children also has recognized the schools as having examples of best practices in early childhood education. Educators in Reggio Emilia refer to the "Pedagogy of Listening," a metaphor for observing carefully the actions, words, and patterns of young children. When one really "listens," one sees the uniqueness, the desires, the interests, and the strengths of the child. This is critical to initiating curriculum and instruction that connects with what children already know and can do and motivates them to pursue further learning.

Listening to young children requires that the adults take on the role of inquirers and data collectors. Adults who study children have opportunities to tap into Vygotsky's (1978) *zone of proximal development* to challenge them. By listening to and documenting what the children are doing, they build upon concrete experiences and help advance their skill level. Two examples clarify this strategy.

Example 1: Building Blocks

John and Bart (two 4-year-old boys) routinely build with blocks together every day. The teachers have been observing how they were playing and negotiating (i.e., who takes which blocks off the shelf and who makes suggestions for the direction of the play). They notice that Bart always followed John's suggestions. On the third day of studying the block play, Bart wants to add a plastic airplane to the structure. The observant teacher then inquires of Bart, "Are you thinking of building an airport out of blocks?" John and Bart both become very excited about the prospect of building a complex airport structure with the control tower, the landing zones, and the places where trucks come and go with suitcases and supplies. For the next 2 days, the boys keep asking their peers and teachers questions about other things they might find in an airport. Bart takes on a leadership role in reporting back to John about other things they should add to their structure. Not only does he gain confidence in his ability to make suggestions and carry them out, but he also begins a project about airports that other children are interested in joining. Each time he adds more to his representation of the airport, he becomes more articulate about the many different facets of an airport. The teachers begin to see strengths and interests in Bart that they had not previously recognized.

Example 2: Gerbil Stories

Kimberly is a first-grade girl who has been focused on her gerbil since the beginning of school. The teacher notices that Kimberly's typical journal writing is a one-page story about the escapades of her gerbil. The teacher gathers several children's stories about animal adventures and reads them aloud to the class. She discusses with the students how authors develop the animal characters in their stories to add interest and intrigue. The teacher then probes Kimberly about her gerbil. Does Kimberly's gerbil know other animals? Does her gerbil ever have any adventures? Kimberly can't wait to enhance her gerbil stories and soon she is writing chapter books about the adventures of her gerbil and other animal characters.

These two examples demonstrate different ways to listen to children. In the first example, teachers' observations and intervention with a question spawned a whole project where the children took on different roles, and growth was fostered in both the social and emotional domain and in the content knowledge of airports. In the second example, the child's writing was stuck in a pattern that inhibited growth. By using the child's interest in her own gerbil and making a connection to the way other authors write about animals, the teacher motivated the student to reach beyond her current level of writing and expand her literacy skills. In both examples, each teacher's intervention was a result of careful listening and a thorough understanding of where the child needed to be challenged. The rationale for such careful listening, observation, and documentation is to provide entry points for teachers to enhance challenge and growth in each child.

Screening and Assessment

In addition to carefully observing and listening, there are more formal ways of assessing students' strengths and needs. The primary purpose of assessment should always be to provide more information for instruction, whether one is looking for talents or weaknesses.

Developmental Screening

In the United States, federal law guarantees free screening for all children, at the age of 3, to be paid for by the child's local public school district. The purpose of this screening is to look for developmental delays or disabilities. There is no similar law for schools to find children who go beyond developmental expectations, although many of the screening instruments provide that type of information. Too numerous to name, such screening tools generally look for developmental milestones in fine and gross motor skills, as well as in vocabulary and speech development, and social and emotional growth. Highly verbal young children generally will test beyond their chronological age on such verbal measurement tools. Some developmental screening instruments also have questionnaires for parents that enable the examiner to gain more culturally relevant information (e.g., whether the child comes from a home where English is the first language) or find out about routines and schedules. What does a parent or a teacher do with information that demonstrates the child is ahead developmentally? The most important outcome of a developmental screening is that it gives guidance as to what the child may need for future instruction. One cannot assume that if a child is ahead on some measures developmentally (e.g., advanced vocabulary) that he or she is ahead on all measures (e.g., fine or gross motor skills). Thus, parents and teachers may want to encourage young children with advanced verbal skills to share their creative stories by talking into a tape recorder instead of expecting them to be able to express their stories in writing. This demonstrates that the strength of the child is highly valued, and the "weaknesses" have not become hindrances because the child is not at the developmental level to write the story with paper and pencil. It is common to find young children frustrated because they have such uneven levels of development (often called *asynchronous development*) that they often imagine what their product should look like, but cannot execute it the way they imagine it. Parents, as well as early childhood educators, need more training in the ways that children's asynchronous development affects their growth and achievement. Often times, teachers and parents have unreasonable expectations of young children because they see one area of growth so far ahead of another.

Standardized Testing

Research supports that parents who suspect their child is gifted often do have children who perform well on intelligence tests. Smutny (2000) stated, "Since about 80% of the parent population can identify their children's giftedness by ages four or five, a short cut to finding these students is to consult with parents" (p. 1). Although knowing a child's IQ may be important information for a parent, it yields little help for the day care provider, the classroom teacher, or the people who come into daily contact with the child. More practical information would include determining what to do with the child to continue to help him or her grow and develop in all domains. NAEYC and the National Association of Early Childhood Specialists and State Departments of Education (NAECS/SDE) have a joint position statement regarding the use of standardized assessments. Primarily, these professional organizations support standardized testing only when it is used to inform instruction. They do not support standardized testing as a means to deny any child access or opportunities for early childhood programs (e.g., kindergarten entry).

Portfolio Collections and Work Sampling Systems

Many early childhood programs have some form of work sampling system in place or a collection of children's work samples in a portfolio representing various domains (e.g., literacy, mathematical thinking, arts and aesthetics, and social and emotional competencies). A portfolio approach to documenting growth gives students opportunities to demonstrate their skills over time. The Work Sampling System (Meisels, 1995) is one example of standardizing the procedure for collecting work samples of children in every content domain. According to Meisels, "This performance assessment system assesses and documents children's skills, knowledge, behavior, and accomplishments as displayed across a wide variety of education domains and as manifested on multiple occasions" (p. 1). In the Work Sampling System, teachers also have a developmental checklist they can use to check off the developmental milestones as they are demonstrated in the children's work samples.

Practical Strategy 4: Assess Continually

The fourth practical strategy when teaching young children is to collect information on an ongoing basis (e.g., daily). Young children are different from older, school-age children in the rate by which they acquire competencies. It is not unusual for an emergent reader to advance three grade levels in one year because decoding words suddenly makes sense to the child. Another example might be a child who learns to print his or her name on one day with substantial help from an adult, and 2 days later, with no help at all. Young children are rapidly changing in almost all domains daily. Therefore, teachers continually must observe, listen, and document demonstrated growth. There are several implications of this strategy. First, teachers should not assume that if children were screened, assessed, or tested over the summer that they will enter the school year with the same skills demonstrated on such assessments. Even if teachers begin the academic year with curriculum-based assessments, they should be cautioned about forming permanent grouping arrangements.

All groups of children in early childhood environments should be flexible. Children should be grouped according to interest, self-made choices, and readiness levels of academic skills. The second implication relates to teacher training and pedagogy. Early childhood teachers, caregivers, and teacher aides need more professional development in observation and documentation skills and more time to collaborate with other teachers to discuss their documentation. Much can be learned from the schools in Reggio Emilia, Italy, where teaching is focused on the study of children, and documentation is fundamental to their pedagogy.

Creating Optimal Early Learning Environments

The role of adults in a child's environment is critical. Young children have many "teachers" in their environment. In fact, young children learn both inappropriate and appropriate behaviors from their teachers. In the broadest sense, teachers include everyone from whom young children learn including caregivers, parents, siblings, peers, and classroom teachers. Parents and classroom teachers have similar and different roles. They are both responsible for creating environments that stimulate the love for learning and nurturing children's strengths and talents. However, the classroom teacher takes on an additional responsibility, which is overseeing the growth of the child in a social setting, one where the child learns to negotiate acceptable behaviors in small and large groups.

The role of the teacher is to create an accepting community of learners where all children are valued, treated with respect, and intentionally challenged. The teacher creates the community structure of the classroom and helps parents understand the value of building a cohesive classroom community.

In Reggio Emilia, they refer to the "environment" as the "third educator" (Rinaldi, 2006, p. 77), but it's the teacher who sets up the environment both physically and emotionally. There are several strategies teachers and parents can use to create an optimal learning environment for young children.

Practical Strategy 5: Create a Literacy-Rich Environment

Literacy is more than reading. A literacy rich environment is one in which children have many opportunities to listen, read, speak, and write. In Duke's (2000) study comparing classrooms in predominately high and low socioeconomic schools, major differences in print experiences and environments were found, favoring high socioeconomic schools. The amount and type of print that children are exposed to and the nature of the students' print experience were investigated. The amount of print was determined by considering the number and variety of reading materials (e.g., books, magazines, and newspapers), the degree to which print was present on walls and other surfaces, and the extent that print was involved in classroom activities. The type of print experienced also was evaluated with reading and writing extended text (narrative forms) considered more desirable than the mere reading of letters, words, phrases, or single sentences (e.g., "the word wall"). Finally, the nature of the print experience was explored by examining the ways in which students were using print. In the literacy-rich environments, students became "agents" of print. They were readers and writers (Duke, 2000).

Therefore, it is not enough just to have books in the house or in the classroom; it is imperative to create an environment where children read and write for authentic purposes. Three-year-olds can have opportunities to ask questions, develop questionnaires, "write" in their journals, label their drawings, tell a story, make shopping lists, "read" to a friend, or listen to a story. Advice to parents to read to their children is well-founded on research (National Literacy Trust, 2001). Reading to young children is positively correlated with higher achievement (Barton & Coley, 1992). Listening to stories read aloud builds children's vocabulary, enhances their realm of experiences, encourages authentic opportunities for discussion and dialogue, and introduces children to the conventions of text and literature. Many young children have special interests that can be encouraged by providing a variety of nonfiction books, as well as fiction, in their environment.

A literacy-rich environment in the home would include a variety of books and print materials. Children should see their parents read and write often. Parents should encourage children to read and write for authentic purposes such as writing a letter to a far-away grandparent, sending an e-mail to a friend, looking up the time of a child's favorite TV show in the newspaper, or adding something to a shopping list. It does not include rote and drill practice on the letters of the alphabet or spending hours trying to help children decode words to read print material that is too difficult for them. Emergent readers should be taught the joy of reading and the possibilities of learning through literature.

It is difficult for children who already know how to read to enter an early childhood program where the teacher uses a reading curriculum that features the "letter of the week." Unfortunately, it is all too common that teachers use prescribed literacy programs that do not differentiate for the advanced reader. However, if teachers follow best practices in writing and reading (Zemelman, Daniels, & Hyde, 1998), children with advanced literacy skills may be challenged. For reading, best practices include giving students many choices of reading material; providing time for independent reading; offering many genres of literature; emphasizing comprehension skills, as opposed to decoding; and providing plenty of opportunities to write before and after reading.

Best practices in writing include giving students choice and ownership in their writing, making writing activities authentic and purposeful, focusing on growth, and giving students opportunities to self-evaluate their work. Most importantly in the early years, writing should focus on expression and not on the standard conventions of writing.

An early childhood classroom that incorporates these best practices may include many literacy activities throughout the day. For example, in the morning during choice time, students may choose from a variety of literacy activities such as writing poetry, riddles, thank-you letters or journals; listening to a story and following along on the computer; and making a list of questions to ask an expert. During instructional reading, students may be grouped according to skill level and respond to a particular book either read by the teacher or themselves. During journal writing time, the teacher moves about the room to conference individually with students as they evaluate their own writing progress. After recess some children have independent quiet reading time while the teacher listens to others read leveled books or novels, depending on their reading level. The teacher gives individual reading instruction and develops shared goals with the students for reading progress during this time. Students then have time to read with a friend (buddy reading). When buddy reading is over, students join a large group to listen to a shared story such as a more difficult chapter book read by the teacher. During an afternoon choice time, children may work with a teacher to write a report about information gained from an independent study to share with other students. In a classroom where best practices in literacy are implemented, reading, writing, speaking, and listening are continuous throughout the day because the teacher provides authentic learning experiences to apply literacy skills.

Practical Strategy 6: Provide Authentic Learning Experiences

Learning experiences are authentic when they are purposeful and meaningful to the student. An example of one such experience is a "daily sign-in question." Students, or the teacher, may generate the daily sign-in question. Generally, it asks for students' opinions about something related to the project they are studying, or it seeks information about the children themselves that can be tallied and analyzed for later investigations. For example, when the preschool students at University Primary

School, an early childhood gifted education program affiliated with the Department of Special Education at the University of Illinois, were investigating music in their homes, they surveyed their parents to find out what types of musical instruments they had at home. The questions that were generated by the students asked parents things like, "Do you have a piano at home?" or "Do you have a guitar?" They discovered that one family had a harmonium and another had a timbale. They invited these parents to be guest experts and share their instruments with the whole class. In addition to collecting the information they needed for their project, students engaged in reading, writing, and math upon arrival at school each day.

After everyone has opportunity to sign in and answer the question, a small group of children might work with a teacher during choice time to analyze and display the results. The results are then shared with the rest of the class during whole group meeting time. Throughout the year, children become experts at tallying surveys and displaying results in ways that can be understood by all children. In the preschool classroom, students use concrete manipulatives for every tally mark so that children understand the one-to-one correspondence of the responses to the bar graph that they are developing both with pen and with manipulatives (e.g., Unifix cubes). Students have "real" motivation to analyze and display their data because they are excited to share their results with the other children in the class. Often, the survey questions spark debates and more questions at large-group time that encourage children to seek answers independently during choice time.

Although not all experiences can be authentic in early childhood classrooms, the majority of learning should take place in natural and authentic contexts. This does not mean that students are always self-initiating what they want to do. On the contrary, teachers who provide authentic contexts for learning have to be more skillful and have to plan in more complex ways to create the environments for children to engage in this way. In addition, teachers need to realize that they are not the only teachers in the classroom. Other children are teachers, too, because learning occurs in social contexts. When children problem solve together, they are learning from one another.

Practical Strategy 7: Provide Choices to Engage in Learning

The best strategy that teachers can use to make learning authentic in their classrooms is to provide a choice time where children have input into their learning activities. All of the choices should be acceptable so that the teacher is not disappointed with students' selections. Kohn (1999) has written a great deal about the benefits of incorporating choice in a child's school day. Choice is important for both high- and low-achieving children. Kohn maintained, "When children believe that they can exert control over success in school, they perform better on cognitive tasks. And when children succeed in school, they are more likely to view school performance as a controllable outcome" (p. 37).

When thinking about what types of choices and how many to have available, teachers may wish to consider the interests of the children, subject domain, and the pragmatics of the choice (e.g., the degree to which adult supervision or certain materials are needed).

In some cases, teachers may have to follow a specific timetable or district requirement (e.g., 90 minutes of literacy activities). In this case, the teacher may have all literacy choices available for children while he or she pursues guided reading activities according to the mandates of the district curriculum. In other instances, a teacher might want to follow a multiple intelligence approach to the choices and offer several options that represent students' strengths in the multiple intelligences (e.g., listening to music with headphones, creating mazes, writing stories). Another consideration when planning the choices is to think about subject domains, and plan so that there is at least one choice in each of the major subject areas of literacy, math, art, science, and social studies. For example, the following choices might be available:

- read with a friend,
- create an observational drawing of a musical instrument the child is studying,
- record the size of a bean plant, or
- develop questions to use when interviewing the owner of the local music store.

Multiple benefits and advantages of scheduling a choice time during the day are summarized below. Choice time:

- increases student motivation,
- provides opportunities to work in preferred learning styles,
- helps students perform better,
- strengthens interest, and
- reinforces disposition to love to learn.

Research has shown students in early child-initiated programs fare better in later years; many of these programs include time for student choice. Further, choice time provides important opportunities for students to work in their interest areas. During this time period, teachers facilitate students' learning by building upon their ideas and interests. The high level of student engagement allows teachers to work with individuals or small groups (e.g., helping children who are struggling or need additional challenge). Choice time is an excellent opportunity for teachers to involve parents or students from higher grades. It is a comfortable time for volunteers to be working with individuals or small groups because all children are engaged in their respective activities and no children feel singled out for their strengths or deficiencies. The choice time fosters students' natural drive to pursue their curiosities and it provides an opportunity for teachers to engage in the learning process with students. Choice time also provides an ideal framework for students to participate in inquiry and long-term project investigations.

Managing the Choice Period

Ideally, choice time should be no shorter than 60 minutes, even in the early childhood classroom. This is quite a contrast to the advice often given to teachers of young children who are encouraged to plan short activities. When students are interested in what they are doing, there is no reason to make the time frames short and quick. On the contrary, the hour-long time block encourages task commitment, depth, and complexity. Students learn to revisit their work over an extended period of time, self-evaluating and attending to suggestions for improvement, thereby enhancing the quality of their work.

Managing choice time takes careful planning by the teachers and adults in the classroom. Often in early childhood classrooms there are aides or volunteers. The teacher needs to make sure that if several people are in the room facilitating different activities, that such activities take place in appropriate areas. For example, if there is only one wet area for messy art projects, the teacher would plan only one messy art project at a time. Generally, if there are at least two adults in the room, it works well to have one adult facilitating a small-group activity while another becomes the "rover," moving about to help children as needed.

Teachers make the false assumption that children will be unable to handle many choices. In reality, teachers are worried about having too many choices at a time. However, the fewer choices there are in the room, the greater number of children that have to be at each choice, and the more susceptible the teacher is to not having enough materials or enough space for children to fit comfortably in the designated area. In reality, the more choices that teachers allow in the room, the higher probability that children will find something they want to pursue and be highly engaged, freeing up the teacher to lead small reading groups or to facilitate project investigations with individuals or small groups of children. For ideas regarding choice options across content areas, see Table 1.

It is important to make children accountable for their time. Reinforce students' efforts by encouraging them to share what they have accomplished. For example, have a whole-group meeting after choice time where individual or small groups of children share what they have accomplished, ask their peers for feedback or suggestions, or simply have a place in the room to display student work. Students will have internal motivation for task completion. The process of sharing their work with other children enhances child-to-child dialogue, critical and evaluative thinking, and reinforces the notion that feedback can be useful to enhance one's ideas. An example of this occurs on a daily basis at University Primary School. In the process of making boxes and junk representations (structures out of recyclable materials), students bring their design problems to the group for suggestions, modeling the authentic way that people work together to achieve common goals. Importantly, children learn to question each other about their ideas, and give constructive feedback. Students become more articulate by explaining their ideas to others and the teacher praises what is valued in the classroom—thinking, problem solving, collaboration, and hard work!

Table 1

Possibilities for Student Choices Across the Content Areas

Ongoing Choices	Literacy	Mathematical Thinking	Project Investigations
Observational drawing (e.g., science center)	Read independently	Collecting Data	List questions about a topic
Use specific computer software:	Read nonfiction	Counting	Develop a survey
	Read with a friend	Graphing	Design an experiment
Kidspiration	Internet search	Surveying	Create representations
Microsoft PowerPoint	Observational drawing	Geo-boards	Interview an expert
Microsoft Word	Write in journals	Measure	Document field experiences
"Boxes and Junk":	Write interview questions	Parquetry blocks	
creating structures out	Write results or reports	Pattern blocks	
of recyclable materials	Write letters	Peg boards	
		Rods	
		Analyze survey results	

Practical Strategy 8: Provide Opportunities for Inquiry

"Children can raise the right question themselves if the setting is right. Once the right question is raised, they are moved to tax themselves to the fullest to find an answer." (Duckworth, 1996)

There are perennial debates in the field of early childhood education about the appropriate curriculum for young children. What is reported most often as best practice is the type of curriculum that allows students to make choices about their learning and to pursue answers to their own questions. Units and themes, although they have the potential to be fun and engaging, do not always satisfy the requirement of being a significant topic for young children. A common early childhood theme such as teddy bears or the rain forest does not give students appropriate first-hand experiences to investigate the world around them. Three curricular approaches designed for young children that include inquiry are the Project Approach (Katz & Chard, 1998, 2000), the Creative Curriculum (Dodge, Colker, & Heroman, 2002), and the approach found in the schools of Reggio Emilia, Italy

(Edwards, Gandini, & Forman, 1998). Renzulli's (1977) Type III independent and small-group investigations is another example of an inquiry-based curricular approach often recommended for gifted students.

The Project Approach

A project as defined by Katz and Chard (2000) is "an in-depth study of a particular topic, usually undertaken by a whole class working on subtopics in small groups, sometimes by a small group of children within a class, and occasionally by an individual child" (p. 2). Projects present learning to children in real-life contexts and integrate the acquisition and application of basic skills through inquiry modes of learning. Topics for project investigations may be part of a required curriculum, determined by state learning standards, or initiated by the interests of the children. Project investigations differ from "projects" and "products," the result of units or theme-based curriculum. As products, teachers may give students options for the types of projects students choose to do related to a thematic topic such as creating a model of a solar system, making a mask of a storybook character, or writing a play with an alternative ending. A project investigation that uses an inquiry approach engages students in firsthand investigations where children ask questions, make predictions, go on field studies to collect data, analyze their data, and share their findings.

Using an inquiry-based approach to curriculum allows teachers to maximize the ways they differentiate the curriculum for students of advanced abilities because students enter into their investigations at their own readiness level and in ways that interest them the most. For example, one classroom had the students engaged in a project entitled, "Who Measures What in Our Neighborhood." Some students were interested in what things get measured, other students were interested in the measuring tools, and some wanted to explore how the measuring tools worked. One first grader was most interested in exploring all of the things that were measured in a car (e.g., gas, mileage, speed). The teacher allowed the student to explore her car's measurement gauges in depth (see http://www.ed.uiuc.edu/ups/curriculum2002/measure/phase2narr.shtml). By using students' own questions as starting points for the study, teachers do not have to predetermine who would benefit most from a particular strategy or level of involvement.

Students' high interest level often impacts what children are motivated to achieve. A kindergarten child who may not know all of his numbers up to 100 may be quite interested in learning more about those numbers when he sees them on a speedometer or a thermometer. Therefore, when thinking about how to differentiate for young children, it is more important to let the child's interest guide the challenge level rather than push the child into content areas that are not relevant or meaningful for the child. When teachers facilitate high-quality project investigations, there are innumerable ways that children can be challenged. For instance, when students investigate topics, they acquire vocabulary of the discipline. When students studied "Who Measures What in Our Neighborhood," they discovered that the water survey office was right behind the school. They investigated all of the instruments that the scientists used to measure rainfall, the water in the ground, and the temperature of the water. Students made representations of the baler, the coil, and the thermometer.

Teachers who must use a district or specified curriculum still may use an inquiry approach to "uncover the topic" with the children. Learning about animal habitats is a popular curricular unit in early childhood classrooms. Following the phases of the project approach, the teachers first would brainstorm all of the essential big ideas that they want to make sure children understand by the end of the investigation. Often these big ideas are found in state learning standards. Then, they may give students several days of activities that allow them to learn about what children already know and understand about habitats. Some activities may include building a topic web with the children's ideas about habitats, drawing experience stories, or giving students opportunities to share their stories about habitats orally during a whole-group meeting. Students may talk about their experiences at a zoo or their own pets and how they care for them. Phase 1 activities provide responses from children that enable teachers to learn about students' current level of understanding before pursuing the inquiry phase of the project. During discussions of habitats in Phase 1, students realize that they have different understandings of habitats and a variety of types of questions they would like to pursue.

To begin Phase 2 of the project, the teacher helps students brainstorm and categorize their questions about habitats into smaller study topics. For example, some students may be most interested in habitats of their pets. Others may be more interested in the habitat they can observe right outside the classroom window. Still other students may want to find out more about the people who study animal habitats and what those people do. Throughout Phase 2 of the project, the teacher facilitates students' firsthand investigations by arranging access to experts, planning field studies, providing materials, and scaffolding students' data collection and research skills. A teacher might differentiate the data collection process by teaching how to use the cross bar to count by fives to the children who already know how to use tally marks to count. Other students may just be beginning to use tally marks, so the teacher could encourage one-to-one correspondence with the objects they are counting and the tally marks they are recording. These examples of how teachers can differentiate instruction within the inquiry process are simply to demonstrate that teachers do not need to separate children to give them the next skills they may need to be challenged. But rather, the teacher who is "listening" and observant will scaffold existing skills within the context of the "work" or the investigation that the child is pursuing, giving the student authentic opportunities to use new skills. Children with various skills will learn from one another as they watch students with different levels of competencies navigate through the inquiry process.

In Phase 3 of the project investigation, teachers provide opportunities for children to design ways to share their findings from Phase 2. There are tremendous opportunities for students to collaborate and brainstorm ideas for sharing information. Teachers may take these opportunities to give direct instruction on technology (use of software such as PowerPoint and Kidspiration), writing reports, creating data displays, or collaborating on group murals.

Working in small groups to share their findings instead of one large class group provides students more authentic reasons to present their data. If every child in the classroom went through the same investigation, there would be no need to share students' findings publicly. By having different study groups, the teacher has created a learning environment where students are motivated to carefully articulate what they have learned so that their peers will learn from them. Often, Phase 3 culminates with the students sharing what they have learned with their families.

The teacher encourages students to engage in self-reflection and self-evaluation during Phase 3 of the project and simultaneously engages in his or her own documentation and evaluation of the students' growth. Typical Phase 3 activities might entail doing a second topic web of what the children know about the topic after the investigation, a simple questionnaire asking the students what they would like to tell a friend about the topic, and sending a survey home to parents to elicit input about their perspectives of their child's learning experience. Throughout the inquiry process, teachers who maximize opportunities for creative and critical thinking use the language of thinking and model the process of inquiry explicitly for the students.

The Creative Curriculum

The Creative Curriculum (Dodge et al., 2002) is a comprehensive approach to planning curriculum for children ages 3–5 that includes resources such as assessment tools, online assessment data management systems, and notebooks with examples of project-based investigations called "study starters."

Each study starter is organized much like investigations in the Project Approach and is comprised of three parts: (1) weekly planning and enhancements geared to interest areas, (2) sample investigations, and (3) further questions to investigate.

First, the teacher determines what students already know about a topic and what they would like to learn more about. For example, children might develop charts and webbings of their thoughts and ideas pertaining to certain topics.

Investigations generally involve small groups of students. According to the developers of the curriculum, "each investigation is based on a question that children may ask" (Teaching Strategies, 2005, p. 14). Content about the topic is integrated into other aspects of the curriculum, and teachers may design choices that relate to the topic of students' investigations.

Following an investigation, students celebrate learning. Much like the Project Approach, a culminating event is planned where children can share what they have learned with others.

Study starters provide specific examples of topics (e.g., boxes, chairs, water pipes, flowers, shadows, and rocks) for teachers who would like to engage their students in project investigations. They guide teachers to think about linkages to state standards, disciplines of study, and students' interest areas. The curriculum also provides a framework for teachers to reflect upon with regard to the children's learning experiences. The inquiry-based instruction is in line with the NAEYC's position on best practices for preschoolers. Readers can refer to the Creative Curriculum Web site for more information on this comprehensive approach (see http://www.teachingstrategies.com).

Reggio Emilia

Project work in Reggio Emilia, Italy, is but one component of the Reggio Emilia philosophy. Gardner (as cited in Edwards et al., 1998) sums up the philosophy by stating, "In Reggio, the teachers know how to listen to children, how to allow them to take initiative, and yet how to guide them in productive ways" (p. xvii).

A prevailing theme in Reggio Emilia is that of the "competent child." Thus, the curriculum is sensitive to the child, emergent and dynamic, to follow the paths the child wants his or her studies to take. The teacher is a researcher and a learner alongside the child, creating the contexts for learning and designing an aesthetic and carefully planned environment as the "third teacher." The teacher provokes thinking and problem solving by organizing the materials in the environment in such a way that stimulates thinking and collaboration. According to Malaguzzi (as cited in Edwards et al., 1998),

> Every year each school delineates a series of related projects, some short range and some long. These themes serve as the main structural supports, but then it is up to the children, the course of events, and the teachers to determine whether the building turns out to be a hut on stilts or an apartment house or whatever. (p. 88)

During the author's last visit to Italy in June 2006, children were observed responding to the newly renovated International Center that was not yet complete. The International Center is a new building in the town of Reggio Emilia designed to host visitors and conferences for people who are interested in the Reggio Emilia approach. Each school or group of children in a school designed ideas for decorating and making the center more comfortable for themselves and visitors. One school focused on how to decorate the columns that were still part of the internal structural supports. In another school, the children designed many different kinds and sizes of chairs to be put into the building. Another group of children focused on the windows and how to cover them. The children's ideas were shared with local artists, and some of their ideas were actually replicated for the finished building. Linking the children to their community is integral to the Reggio Emilia approach.

Another important feature of the Reggio Emilia approach is the "Hundred Languages of Children." This is a metaphor for the many ways that children express themselves. In Reggio Emilia, the schools hire a graphic artist (atelierista) to work with small groups of students in an art studio (atelier) to explore a variety of types of media to enhance their representational skills. Every classroom has a mini-atelier (small art studio) where teachers provide a multitude of materials for children to explore and use to represent their ideas. Creativity and self-expression are salient goals of the Reggio Emilia approach. The hundred languages of children address the diversity of learners and the incorporation of multiple intelligences into the theoretical framework for curriculum delivery. See Hertzog (2001) or Kang (2007) for firsthand descriptions of the Reggio Emilia Approach. The reader can gain a broad array of information from the Web site of the foundation, Friends of Reggio Children (see http://zerosei. comune.re.it/inter/reggiochildren.htm). Because the approach values the uniqueness and the competencies of the young child, it is an appropriate way to serve children with advanced skills and abilities, as well as children who may have disabilities.

Renzulli's Enrichment Triad Model

Renzulli's Type III investigation is well known in the field of gifted education as the third tier of the Enrichment Triad Model (Renzulli, 1977). The theory behind the Enrichment Triad Model is that all children benefit from participating in exploratory activities (Type I Enrichment) and from learning how to develop investigative and research skills (Type II Enrichment), but the third type of enrichment is perhaps most suitable for gifted and talented students. Type III enrichment engages students in firsthand inquiry. They may self-select a topic in their interest area and find out more about it through field work. This model usually is used in elementary programs, and little has been written as to how it has been applied to preschool settings. According to Renzulli (1977), the goals of these types of activities include:

- providing opportunities to apply interests, knowledge, creative ideas, and task commitment to a selective problem;

- acquiring advanced-level understanding of knowledge (content) and methodology (process);
- developing authentic products;
- developing self-directed learning skills in the areas of planning, organization, resource utilization, time management, decision-making, and self-evaluation; and
- developing task commitment, self-confidence, and feelings of creative accomplishment.

Students pursuing Type III investigations become producers of knowledge rather than consumers, actively formulating a problem, designing research, and presenting a product. Renzulli (1977) emphasized that students should emulate professional investigators and select appropriate audiences for final products. Several parallels between the Project Approach and the Type III individual or small-group investigation can be made (Hertzog, 1999). Both have students actively engaged in pursuing answers to their own questions, and both provide students opportunities to become creative producers, especially when they design ways to share their findings. For young children, however, families may be the most appropriate and authentic audience with which they can share their work.

To summarize, the curricular models or approaches described have common elements based on best pedagogical practices for young students:

- They are based on how young children learn best—through firsthand experiences.
- They are sensitive and responsive to the interests of children.
- They engage students in some form of inquiry, affording them the opportunity to seek answers to their own questions.
- They provide opportunities for students to collect, analyze, and represent their data, giving them authentic opportunities to integrate and apply basic skills.

- They provide opportunities for students to think critically and creatively.

Most importantly, the adults who work with children have an opportunity to learn more about them, to learn alongside them, and to nurture the disposition to inquire, which will prepare them for lifelong learning in our ever changing world.

Practical Strategy 9: Make Explicit the Language of Thinking

Effective teachers probe and engage all children in higher levels of thinking. When engaged in project investigations, young children are taught to analyze, synthesize, and evaluate their data. They also are taught to predict and hypothesize based on their predictions. Tishman and Perkins (1997) presented several ways to conceptualize the "language of thinking" and offered vocabulary for teachers to explicitly use "thinking words" in their instruction. They stated:

Using the language of thinking in the classroom helps develop learners' sensitivity to occasions for engaging in high-level thinking. Terms like *claim*, *option*, *opinion*, *guess*, and *doubt* alert learners to opportunities to do such things as probe an assumption, seek evidence, identify reasons, or look at a problem from a new point of view. (p. 372)

Tishman and Perkins (1997) denoted the three categories of language related to thinking as: (1) claim to knowledge, (2) intellectual process, and (3) kinds of ideas or outcomes. Table 2 provides examples of words that teachers can use and model for children to alert them to when they are making a claim to know something, when they are thinking about an idea, or when they are presenting their ideas.

When teachers are facilitating project investigations, they have multiple opportunities to use the language of thinking.

Table 2
Language of Thinking

Claim to Knowledge	conjecture, conclude, believe, confirm, doubt, know, suggest, speculate, suspect, and theorize
Intellectual Process	analyze, contemplate, discern, interpret, investigate, ponder, examine, and recollect
Kinds of Ideas or Outcomes	conclusion, hypothesis, option, solution, reason, claim, and theory

Note. Adapted from *The Language of Thinking*, by S. Tishman and D. Perkins, 1997, *Phi Delta Kappan, 78*, 368–374.

Before all field trips, they ask students to *predict* what they will see. When they design an experiment with children, they ask them to *hypothesize* about the outcome. Teachers ask students to *draw conclusions* from their investigation. They may ask a child what he or she is *pondering* or *wondering*. During discussions, the teachers may ask students to support their conclusions with *evidence*. To encourage critical analysis, teachers should expect and allow for students to argue with each other about their ideas. Tishman and Perkins (1997) stated, "Frequent exposure to the language of argumentation, such terms as premise, reason, conclusion, evidence, theory, and hypothesis, draws learners into the values and commitments of critical analysis" (p. 372).

Modeling the language of thinking places value on the thinking process. Teachers give the clear message that students' processes of thinking are highly valued and respected. The emphasis is shifted from being "right" or "correct" about something, to having reasons and evidence to support their ideas. Students go beyond recalling the answers that teachers are expecting as signs of learning in more traditional approaches.

Parents, too, can model the language of thinking in their everyday interactions with their children. They can ask their children what they are wondering. They can model their own thinking processes when they are making decisions, and they can encourage their children to support their ideas and arguments with theories, reasons, or beliefs. Parents should praise their young children for thinking about alternatives and possibilities, for giving arguments, and for engaging in higher level thought processes.

Five strategies to optimize the learning environment for young children have been presented:

1. create a literacy-rich environment,
2. provide authentic learning experiences,
3. allow choices to engage in learning,
4. afford opportunities for inquiry, and
5. make explicit the language of thinking.

These strategies can be used in the home, as well as in early learning centers or classrooms. In classrooms, it is beneficial to have a high teacher-to-student ratio so that children will have plenty of opportunities to interact with and be guided by adults. Materials should be varied and accessible so that students have multiple options to express their ideas. Documenting children's work enhances the visibility of their thinking processes and enables students to revisit their ideas. Finally, encouraging students to reflect, self-evaluate, and add on to their work empowers them with tools for lifelong learning.

Clearly, there are more strategies that could be added to this list. But, the ones discussed here encompass what we know about how children grow, develop, and learn.

Current Issues in Early Childhood Gifted Education

Child development and cognitive psychology have greatly influenced practices in early childhood gifted education. Based on principles from these areas of study, NAEYC has published standards for quality of early childhood programs. To be a NAEYC accredited program, the physical environment, curriculum, staff, and administration all must meet defined criteria for quality. To summarize, high-quality programs have safe and aesthetic learning environments, well-qualified staff, ongoing plans for professional development, adequately paid workers, appropriate assessment, curriculum and instruction, and supportive structures for family involvement. The accreditation criteria are easy to access from the NAEYC Web site (see http://www.naeyc.org/accreditation).

The Early Childhood Division of the National Association for Gifted Children (NAGC) has a position statement that also articulates core elements that must be included in early education environments. The core elements address many of the topics discussed earlier, including the environment, pedagogy, and curriculum. Two of the core elements explicitly express the importance of teaching children in an environment with a diverse population of students:

- interaction and collaboration with diverse peer groups of children having like and different interests and abilities, and
- opportunities for social interaction with same-age peers as well as individuals with similar cognitive abilities and interests (NAGC, 2006, p. 2).

Giving students opportunities to learn with a diverse group of peers is an important component of early childhood education.

Practical Strategy 10: Celebrate Diversity

One of the most critical issues in American schools today is the increasing diversity of the student population. According to federal statistics:

The racial diversity of children under age 18 in the United States changed significantly from 1990 to 2000. The percentage of white children has decreased from 74.9% to 68.6%; while the percentage of Hispanic children has increased from 12.2% to 17.1%. (NAEYC, 2000, ¶ 1)

Teachers are unprepared to understand, accept, or use to their advantage the multicultural backgrounds of their students. Children from differing cultures bring multiple perspectives to the learning environment, so the diversity of students should be celebrated.

Teachers should create warm inclusive environments where all students and teachers are learners, and where all students have opportunities to share what they know and can do well. In an early childhood classroom, activities that demonstrate diversity are valued and include (but are not limited to) the following:

- label important objects and places in the room with different languages,

- provide children's books in a variety of languages in the class library,
- listen to music and teach songs from other cultures,
- include snacks from other cultures,
- invite parents to share their family traditions throughout the year,
- have a map that shows where the children's families lived before coming to the United States,
- encourage becoming pen pals with children from another place such as a day care center, city, or country,
- use live video feeds to explore places remote to one's own city, and
- if possible, give English-speaking students opportunities to learn a second language.

Head Start programs were founded upon deficit principles. Educators tried to provide what they thought children were deprived of having in their own homes—a head start to school learning. Early childhood learning environments should be established from a strength-based, not deficit-based, principle. Appreciate what students from diverse linguistic and cultural backgrounds know and can do, and allow them to grow from those roots. Give them confidence in their own abilities so they will seek challenging learning opportunities, and provide all students in the class with the options for choice and growth.

Inclusive Education

Because giftedness frequently is measured only by tests of intelligence, very few programs identify preschoolers as gifted and serve them separately from nongifted peers. Instead, most young gifted children are in inclusive early childhood environments, and prior to kindergarten, are in private preschools. Although there is an emerging call for universal preschools, these district- and state-funded programs prioritize children with disabilities or those who are at-risk for school failure.

Inclusive early childhood settings can provide a basis for learning respect, social justice, and tolerance of the uniqueness of others. Important ethical and moral values begin at home and carry into students' early childhood settings, whether they are home day care, public day care centers, or early elementary classrooms. The tolerance and respect for others must be taught early and in all settings.

The type of challenging inquiry-based curriculum described earlier allows for children with all abilities to pursue their interests at their own readiness levels. Thus, all children can benefit from such pedagogy, and it is not necessary to separate them in order to serve them well. If teachers appreciate the uniqueness of each child, they will find ways to engage and challenge even their most talented learners. More importantly, teachers will tap into the potential of those talents and abilities that have not yet been realized. The flexible grouping that happens continually as children make choices about their own learning is another way that enables teachers to provide time for gifted or talented children to pursue learning in depth and with a greater intensity than their peers.

Challenging Behaviors

A second issue facing early childhood educators is the rise of what has been termed "challenging behaviors." Many children get expelled from early childhood centers or kindergarten because of their poor behaviors (Gilliam & Shahar, 2006). Even very bright children may have difficult behaviors. Their social and emotional competencies are not at the same level as their academic expertise. The Center on the Social and Emotional Foundations for Learning (CSEFL) has a number of professional development materials for teachers to help them reduce challenging behaviors in the classroom. Not surprisingly, their strongest recommendation for developing a foundation for children is to develop positive relationships with the children themselves. Teachers who follow the strategies of valuing student competencies, appreciating each student's uniqueness, and becoming "listeners" will undoubtedly get to know their students well and develop positive relationships. They will be able to intervene before behavior gets out of control, and they also will be able to arrange the environment in ways that engage most children so disruptive behaviors will be minimized. Students who are internally motivated to learn do not need external systems of rewards. Creating the environment that optimally engages students can greatly reduce challenging behaviors.

Asperger's Syndrome

More and more children are finding themselves in classrooms with students with disabilities. The number of students with autism has been increasing rapidly in the United States. The Autism Society of America (ASA; 2007b) reports:

> A 2007 Centers for Disease Control report found that 1 in 150 children in America today have an autism spectrum disorder (ASD). ASA estimates that 1.5 million Americans and their families are now affected. Autism is a national health crisis, costing the U.S. at least $35 billion annually. (¶ 1)

Although there still is disagreement as to whether or not Asperger's syndrome (AS) is a form of autism, more and more children have been diagnosed with Asperger's. According to the Autism Society of America (2007a), the "diagnosis of Asperger's Disorder is on the increase although it is unclear whether it is more prevalent or whether more professionals are detecting it" (¶ 9).

This has impacted the field of early childhood gifted education because children with AS often have advanced vocabulary and language skills. According to the National Institute of Neurological Disorders and Stroke (2007),

> The most distinguishing symptom of AS is a child's obsessive interest in a single object or topic to the exclusion of any other. Children with AS want to know everything

about their topic of interest and their conversations with others will be about little else. Their expertise, high level of vocabulary, and formal speech patterns make them seem like little professors. (¶ 2)

When these children get referred for special education services, their Individualized Education Programs (IEPs) often are written to improve their social skills. They also need to receive services for their strengths in language. Their strong interests may be used as starting points to develop and strengthen their social skills. For example, a child with Asperger's syndrome who is interested in every capital of the United States might use that information to engage with other children by developing a questionnaire asking his or her peers what city they were born in or in what states their parents have lived. Even though specialists in gifted education often do not serve on IEP committees, parents and early childhood educators need to be vigilant and advocate for services to meet their needs in their strength areas, as well as their deficits.

In summary, teachers and parents must celebrate and appreciate the diversity that includes children with disabilities and children who speak English as a second language. There is potential talent in all of those children and it is the teacher's role to nurture and develop it. Unfortunately, educators who work with young children often are the least educated, the most underpaid, and the most transient in their professions. The future of our talented young children depends on the quality of our teachers and their dedication to the profession.

As we plan for the future of early childhood gifted education, we must develop new strategies to improve the quality of our teacher and parent education programs. We must envision ways that support our early childhood professionals and value their work.

Summary and Conclusion

"And when children's ideas, rather than being taken seriously, are simply scanned for correspondence to what the teacher wants, well then it isn't too hard to figure out what happens to children's curiosity and resourcefulness later in their childhood." (Duckworth, 1996, as cited in Kohn, 1999, p. 49)

The strategies described in this volume, based on theory and research, are practical because they can be implemented now and with few resources. They are applicable to parents, as well as educators. They are designed to facilitate the growth and development of young children. Early childhood educators should:

- value the competencies of the young child,
- appreciate and enjoy the uniqueness of the young child,
- become "listeners" of young children,
- assess children's learning continually,
- create a literacy-rich environment,
- provide authentic learning experiences,
- allow choices to engage in learning,
- afford opportunities for inquiry,

- make explicit the language of thinking, and
- celebrate diversity.

The importance of giving students the best possible opportunities when they are in their critical years of development is well documented. Teachers and parents play significant roles to guide and nurture their growth and development. Implementing these strategies will empower children to pursue their natural zest for learning and to develop their gifts and talents.

Author's Note

The author used examples based on her experiences as a teacher and a director of University Primary School, an early childhood gifted education program affiliated with the University of Illinois at Urbana-Champaign. She also has seen these strategies and types of activities used successfully in other settings.

References

Anonymous. (2007). Alex's gifts. *Gifted Child Today, 30*(3), 40–41, 65.

Autism Society of America. (2007a). *Asperger's disorder.* Retrieved July 5, 2007, from http://www.autism-society.org/site/PageServer?pagename=about_whatis_asperger

Autism Society of America. (2007b). *Improving the lives of all affected by autism.* Retrieved July 5, 2007, from http://www.autism-society.org

Barton, P. E., & Coley, R. J. (1992). *America's smallest school: The family.* Princeton, NJ: Educational Testing Service.

Dodge, D. T., Coker, L. J., & Heroman, C. (2002). *The creative curriculum* (4th ed.). Washington, DC: Teaching Strategies.

Duckworth, E. (1996). *"The having of wonderful ideas" and other essays on teaching and learning.* New York: Teachers College Press.

Duke, N. (2000). For the rich it's richer: Print experiences and environments offered to children in very low- and very high-socioeconomic status first-grade classrooms. *American Educational Research Journal, 37,* 441–478.

Dweck, C. (2006). *Mindset: The psychology of success.* New York: Random House.

Edwards, C., Gandini, L., & Forman, G. (1998). *The hundred languages of children: The Reggio Emilia approach—advanced reflections* (2nd ed.). Greenwich, CT: Ablex.

Feinburg, S., & Mindess, M. (1994). *Eliciting children's full potential: Designing and evaluating developmentally based programs for young children.* Pacific Grove, CA: Brooks/Cole.

Frances A. Karnes Center for Gifted Studies. (n.d.). *Reaching potential: Recognizing, understanding and serving gifted preschoolers.* [Brochure]. Hattiesburg, MS: Author. Retrieved December 15, 2007, from http://www.usm.edu/gifted/ gifted_preschoolers.html

Gilliam, W. S., & Shahar, G. (2006). Prekindergarten expulsion and suspension: Rates and predictors in one state. *Infants and Young Children, 19,* 228–245.

Hertzog, N. B. (1999). Gifted education in an early childhood context: A secret we should share. In N. L. Hafenstein & B. Walker (Eds.), *Perspectives in gifted education: Young gifted children* (pp. 36–49). Denver, CO: Institute for the Development of Gifted Education.

Hertzog, N. B. (2001, Spring). Reflections and impressions from Reggio: "It's not about art!" *Early Childhood Research and Practice, 3*(1). Retrieved January 4, 2008, from http://ecrp. uiuc.edu/v3n1/hertzog.html

Kang, J. (2007). How many languages can Reggio children speak? Many more than one hundred! *Gifted Child Today, 30*(3), 45–48, 64.

Kantrowitz, B., & Wingert, P. (1991, December 2). Society: The 10 best schools in the world. *Newsweek,* pp. 60–64.

Katz, L., & Chard, S. (1998). *Issues in selecting topics for projects.* Champaign, IL: ERIC Clearinghouse on Elementary and Early Childhood Education. (Eric Document Reproduction Service No. ED424031)

Katz, L., & Chard, S. (2000). *Engaging children's minds: The project approach* (2nd ed.). Norwood, NJ: Ablex.

Kohn, A. (1999). *The schools our children deserve: Moving beyond traditional classrooms and "tougher standards."* Boston: Houghton Mifflin.

Leigh, K. (2007). Joseph. *Gifted Child Today, 30*(3), 40–41, 65.

Meisels, S. J. (1995). *Performance assessment in early childhood education: The work sampling system.* Urbana, IL: ERIC Clearinghouse on Elementary and Early Childhood Education. (ERIC Document Reproduction Service No. ED382407)

National Association for Gifted Children. (2006). *NAGC position paper on early childhood: Creating contexts for individualized learning in early childhood education.* Retrieved February 1, 2007, from http://www.nagc.org/uploadedFiles/PDF/Position_Statement_PDFs/Early%20Childhood%20PositionFinal.pdf

National Association for the Education of Young Children. (2000). *Critical facts about young children and early childhood programs in the United States.* Retrieved July 4, 2007, from http://www.naeyc.org/ece/critical/facts1.asp

National Institute of Neurological Disorders and Stroke. (2007). *NINDS Asperger syndrome information page.* Retrieved July 5, 2007, from http://www.ninds.nih.gov/disorders/asperger/asperger.htm

National Literacy Trust. (2001, May). *Parental involvement and literacy achievement: The research evidence and the way forward.* London: Author. (ERIC Document Reproduction Service No. ED471428)

Renzulli, J. (1977). *The Enrichment Triad Model: Guide for developing defensible programs for the gifted and talented.* Mansfield Center, CT: Creative Learning Press.

Rinaldi, C. (2006). *In dialogue with Reggio Emilia: Listening, researching, and learning.* London: Routledge.

Smutny, J. (2000). *Teaching young gifted children in the regular classroom.* Reston, VA: ERIC Clearinghouse on Disabilities and Gifted Education. (ERIC Document Reproduction No. ED445422).

Teaching Strategies. (2005). *The creative curriculum study starters.* Washington, DC: Author.

Tishman, S., & Perkins, D. (1997). The language of thinking. *Phi Delta Kappan, 78,* 368–374.

Vygotsky, L. S. (1978). *Mind in society.* Boston: Harvard University Press.

Zemelman, S., Daniels, H., & Hyde, A. (1998). *Best practice: New standards for teaching and learning in America's schools.* Portsmouth, NH: Heinemann.

Additional Resources

Web Sites

Center on the Social and Emotional Foundations for Early Learning (CSEFEL)
http://www.vanderbilt.edu/csefel

The Center on the Social and Emotional Foundations for Early Learning is intended to promote the social-emotional outcomes and enhance the school readiness of low-income children birth to age 5, and to serve as a national resource center for disseminating research and evidence-based practices to Head Start and Child Care programs across the country. CSEFEL is jointly funded by the Office of Head Start and Child Care Bureau, under the auspices of the Administration on Children, Youth and Families at the U.S. Department of Health and Human Services.

Early Childhood and Parenting Collaborative at the University of Illinois at Urbana–Champaign

http://ecap.crc.uiuc.edu

This site has a wealth of resources for parents and teachers of young children, including the Clearinghouse on Early Education and Parenting (CEEP), which has archived ERIC digests on early childhood education.

National Association for Gifted Children

http://www.nagc.org

This site has the most comprehensive information for parents and teachers regarding the growth and development of gifted children, as well as resources for gifted education. There is a special highlight of young gifted children linked to the Hot Topics site: Young Gifted: Potential and Promise (http://www.nagc.org/index.aspx?id=1467).

National Association for the Education of Young Children (NAEYC)

http://www.naeyc.org

This site includes standards for accreditation of early childhood programs, resources for parents and teachers of young children, publications, and upcoming professional development opportunities. It is the largest professional organization for the education of young children in the world.

Additional Early Childhood Publications

Avery, C. (1993). . . .*And with a light touch: Learning about reading, writing, and teaching with first graders*. Portsmouth, NH: Heinemann.

Bredekamp, S., & Rosegrant, T. (Eds.). (1995). *Reaching potentials: Transforming early childhood curriculum and assessment, Vol. 2*. Washington, DC: National Association for the Education of Young Children.

Fisher, B. (1995). *Thinking and learning together.* Portsmouth, NH: Heinemann.

Helm, J. H., & Katz, L. (2001). *Young investigators.* New York: Teachers College Press.

Kostelnik, M. J., Soderman, A. K., & Whiren, A. P. (1999). *Developmentally appropriate curriculum: Best practices in early childhood education* (2nd ed.). Upper Saddle River, NJ: Prentice-Hall.

Meier, D. (1995). *The power of their ideas.* Boston: Beacon.

Routman, R. (1991). *Invitations: Changing as teachers and learners K–12.* Portsmouth, NH: Heinemann.

Nancy B. Hertzog received her master's degree in gifted education under the tutelage of Joseph Renzulli at the University of Connecticut and her Ph.D. in special education under the direction of Merle B. Karnes at the University of Illinois at Urbana-Champaign. She currently is an associate professor in the Department of Special Education and the director of University Primary School at the University of Illinois at Urbana-Champaign. Her research focuses on curricular approaches and teaching strategies designed to differentiate instruction and challenge children with diverse abilities. Specifically, she has studied teachers' implementation of the Project Approach in classrooms with both high-achieving and low-achieving children. She has written Web-based curricular guides that detail project investigations of preschool, kindergarten, and first-grade students that have won national recognition from the National Association for Gifted Children (http://www.ed.uiuc.edu/ups/projects). Dr. Hertzog has received grants to integrate technology into early childhood settings.

Dr. Hertzog has been the chair of the Early Childhood Division of the National Association for Gifted Children and served as cochair of the Education Commission of the National Association for Gifted Children. She has published in the *Journal of Curriculum Studies*, *Gifted Child Quarterly*, *Journal for the Education of the Gifted*, *Roeper Review*, *Teaching Exceptional Children*, *Early Childhood Research and Practice*, and *Young Exceptional Children*. She was the guest editor of a special issue on Early Childhood Education for *Gifted Child Today*. She may be reached at the Department of Special Education, 1310 S. Sixth Street, Champaign, IL 61820; nhertzog@uiuc.edu.

Printed in the United States
by Baker & Taylor Publisher Services